MW01167478

This
FISHING
-----LOGBOOK
Belongs to:

_____

ADDRESS: _____

_____

_____

CONTACT NUMBER/S: _____

_____

BOAT NAME: _____

MAKE & MODEL: _____

_____

_____

DESCRIPTION: _____

_____

_____

IN CASE OF EMERGENCY CONTACT:

NAME: _____

_____

CONTACT NUMBER/S: _____

_____

_____

2019

FISHING SCHEDULE
-CALENDAR-

amazon.com/author/safsjdesign

January
Su	Mo	Tu	We	Th	Fr	Sa
		1	2	3	4	5
6	7	8	9	10	11	12
13	14	15	16	17	18	19
20	21	22	23	24	25	26
27	28	29	30	31		

February
Su	Mo	Tu	We	Th	Fr	Sa
					1	2
3	4	5	6	7	8	9
10	11	12	13	14	15	16
17	18	19	20	21	22	23
24	25	26	27	28		

March
Su	Mo	Tu	We	Th	Fr	Sa
					1	2
3	4	5	6	7	8	9
10	11	12	13	14	15	16
17	18	19	20	21	22	23
24	25	26	27	28	29	30
31						

April
Su	Mo	Tu	We	Th	Fr	Sa
	1	2	3	4	5	6
7	8	9	10	11	12	13
14	15	16	17	18	19	20
21	22	23	24	25	26	27
28	29	30				

May
Su	Mo	Tu	We	Th	Fr	Sa
			1	2	3	4
5	6	7	8	9	10	11
12	13	14	15	16	17	18
19	20	21	22	23	24	25
26	27	28	29	30	31	

June
Su	Mo	Tu	We	Th	Fr	Sa
						1
2	3	4	5	6	7	8
9	10	11	12	13	14	15
16	17	18	19	20	21	22
23	24	25	26	27	28	29
30						

July
Su	Mo	Tu	We	Th	Fr	Sa
	1	2	3	4	5	6
7	8	9	10	11	12	13
14	15	16	17	18	19	20
21	22	23	24	25	26	27
28	29	30	31			

August
Su	Mo	Tu	We	Th	Fr	Sa
				1	2	3
4	5	6	7	8	9	10
11	12	13	14	15	16	17
18	19	20	21	22	23	24
25	26	27	28	29	30	31

September
Su	Mo	Tu	We	Th	Fr	Sa
1	2	3	4	5	6	7
8	9	10	11	12	13	14
15	16	17	18	19	20	21
22	23	24	25	26	27	28
29	30					

October
Su	Mo	Tu	We	Th	Fr	Sa
		1	2	3	4	5
6	7	8	9	10	11	12
13	14	15	16	17	18	19
20	21	22	23	24	25	26
27	28	29	30	31		

November
Su	Mo	Tu	We	Th	Fr	Sa
					1	2
3	4	5	6	7	8	9
10	11	12	13	14	15	16
17	18	19	20	21	22	23
24	25	26	27	28	29	30

December
Su	Mo	Tu	We	Th	Fr	Sa
1	2	3	4	5	6	7
8	9	10	11	12	13	14
15	16	17	18	19	20	21
22	23	24	25	26	27	28
29	30	31				

January 1: New Year's Day. January 21: Martin Luther King Day. February 18: Presidents' Day. May 27: Memorial Day.
July 4: Independence Day. September 2: Labor Day. October 14: Columbus Day.
November 11: Veterans Day. November 28: Thanksgiving Day. December 25: Christmas Day

Data provided 'as is' without warranty

2020

amazon.com/author/safsjdesign

January
Su	Mo	Tu	We	Th	Fr	Sa
			1	2	3	4
5	6	7	8	9	10	11
12	13	14	15	16	17	18
19	20	21	22	23	24	25
26	27	28	29	30	31	

February
Su	Mo	Tu	We	Th	Fr	Sa
						1
2	3	4	5	6	7	8
9	10	11	12	13	14	15
16	17	18	19	20	21	22
23	24	25	26	27	28	29

March
Su	Mo	Tu	We	Th	Fr	Sa
1	2	3	4	5	6	7
8	9	10	11	12	13	14
15	16	17	18	19	20	21
22	23	24	25	26	27	28
29	30	31				

April
Su	Mo	Tu	We	Th	Fr	Sa
			1	2	3	4
5	6	7	8	9	10	11
12	13	14	15	16	17	18
19	20	21	22	23	24	25
26	27	28	29	30		

May
Su	Mo	Tu	We	Th	Fr	Sa
					1	2
3	4	5	6	7	8	9
10	11	12	13	14	15	16
17	18	19	20	21	22	23
24	25	26	27	28	29	30
31						

June
Su	Mo	Tu	We	Th	Fr	Sa
	1	2	3	4	5	6
7	8	9	10	11	12	13
14	15	16	17	18	19	20
21	22	23	24	25	26	27
28	29	30				

July
Su	Mo	Tu	We	Th	Fr	Sa
			1	2	3	4
5	6	7	8	9	10	11
12	13	14	15	16	17	18
19	20	21	22	23	24	25
26	27	28	29	30	31	

August
Su	Mo	Tu	We	Th	Fr	Sa
						1
2	3	4	5	6	7	8
9	10	11	12	13	14	15
16	17	18	19	20	21	22
23	24	25	26	27	28	29
30	31					

September
Su	Mo	Tu	We	Th	Fr	Sa
		1	2	3	4	5
6	7	8	9	10	11	12
13	14	15	16	17	18	19
20	21	22	23	24	25	26
27	28	29	30			

October
Su	Mo	Tu	We	Th	Fr	Sa
				1	2	3
4	5	6	7	8	9	10
11	12	13	14	15	16	17
18	19	20	21	22	23	24
25	26	27	28	29	30	31

November
Su	Mo	Tu	We	Th	Fr	Sa
1	2	3	4	5	6	7
8	9	10	11	12	13	14
15	16	17	18	19	20	21
22	23	24	25	26	27	28
29	30					

December
Su	Mo	Tu	We	Th	Fr	Sa
		1	2	3	4	5
6	7	8	9	10	11	12
13	14	15	16	17	18	19
20	21	22	23	24	25	26
27	28	29	30	31		

January 1: New Year's Day. January 20: Martin Luther King Day. February 17: Presidents' Day. May 25: Memorial Day.
July 3: Independence Day (obs.). July 4: Independence Day. September 7: Labor Day. October 12: Columbus Day.
November 11: Veterans Day. November 26: Thanksgiving Day. December 25: Christmas Day

Data provided 'as is' without warranty

amazon.com/author/safsjdesign

LOCATION:	
SWIM:	
START DATE:	END DATE:
TIME:	TIME:
WEATHER:	
BAROMETER:	
AIR TEMP:	WATER TEMP: CC
TIDE:	MOON: J) 0

	RIG	BAIT
ROD 1:		
ROD2:		
ROD3:		
ROD4:		

DATE/TIME	ROD	BITE	FISH	WEIGHT

NOTES: _____

_____

_____

_____

_____

_____

_____

_____

_____

_____

_____

PHOTO DETAILS:

LOCATION:	
SWIM:	
START DATE:	END DATE:
TIME:	TIME:
WEATHER:	
BAROMETER:	
AIR TEMP:	WATER TEMP: CC
TIDE:	MOON: J) 0

	RIG	BAIT
ROD 1:		
ROD2:		
ROD3:		
ROD4:		

DATE/TIME	ROD	BITE	FISH	WEIGHT

NOTES:_____

_____

_____

_____

_____

_____

_____

_____

_____

_____

_____

_____

PHOTO DETAILS:

		LOCATION:		

LOCATION:				
SWIM:				
START DATE:		END DATE:		
TIME:		TIME:		
WEATHER:				
BAROMETER:				
AIR TEMP:		WATER TEMP:		CC
TIDE:		MOON:	J) 0	

	RIG	BAIT
ROD 1:		
ROD2:		
ROD3:		
ROD4:		

DATE/TIME	ROD	BITE	FISH	WEIGHT

NOTES:_____

_____

_____

_____

_____

_____

_____

_____

_____

_____

_____

_____

PHOTO DETAILS:

LOCATION:		
SWIM:		
START DATE:	END DATE:	
TIME:	TIME:	
WEATHER:		
BAROMETER:		
AIR TEMP:	WATER TEMP:	℃
TIDE:	MOON:	J) 0

	RIG	BAIT
ROD 1:		
ROD2:		
ROD3:		
ROD4:		

DATE/TIME	ROD	BITE	FISH	WEIGHT

NOTES:_____

_____

_____

_____

_____

_____

_____

_____

_____

_____

_____

_____

PHOTO DETAILS:

LOCATION:		
SWIM:		
START DATE:	END DATE:	
TIME:	TIME:	
WEATHER:		
BAROMETER:		
AIR TEMP:	WATER TEMP:	℃
TIDE:	MOON:	J) 0

	RIG	BAIT
ROD 1:		
ROD2:		
ROD3:		
ROD4:		

DATE/TIME	ROD	BITE	FISH	WEIGHT

NOTES: _____

_____

_____

_____

_____

_____

_____

_____

_____

_____

_____

_____

PHOTO DETAILS:

LOCATION:		
SWIM:		
START DATE:	END DATE:	
TIME:	TIME:	
WEATHER:		
BAROMETER:		
AIR TEMP:	WATER TEMP:	℃
TIDE:	MOON:	J) 0

	RIG	BAIT
ROD 1:		
ROD2:		
ROD3:		
ROD4:		

DATE/TIME	ROD	BITE	FISH	WEIGHT

NOTES:_____

_____

_____

_____

_____

_____

_____

_____

_____

_____

_____

_____

PHOTO DETAILS:

LOCATION:		
SWIM:		
START DATE:	END DATE:	
TIME:	TIME:	
WEATHER:		
BAROMETER:		
AIR TEMP:	WATER TEMP:	℃
TIDE:	MOON:	J) 0

	RIG	BAIT
ROD 1:		
ROD2:		
ROD3:		
ROD4:		

DATE/TIME	ROD	BITE	FISH	WEIGHT

NOTES: _____

_____

_____

_____

_____

_____

_____

_____

_____

_____

_____

_____

PHOTO DETAILS:

LOCATION:	
SWIM:	
START DATE:	END DATE:
TIME:	TIME:
WEATHER:	
BAROMETER:	
AIR TEMP:	WATER TEMP: ℃
TIDE:	MOON: J) 0

	RIG	BAIT
ROD 1:		
ROD2:		
ROD3:		
ROD4:		

DATE/TIME	ROD	BITE	FISH	WEIGHT

NOTES: _____
_____
_____
_____
_____
_____
_____
_____
_____
_____
_____
_____
_____
_____

PHOTO DETAILS:

LOCATION:	
SWIM:	
START DATE:	END DATE:
TIME:	TIME:
WEATHER:	
BAROMETER:	
AIR TEMP:	WATER TEMP: ℃
TIDE:	MOON: J) 0

	RIG	BAIT
ROD 1:		
ROD2:		
ROD3:		
ROD4:		

DATE/TIME	ROD	BITE	FISH	WEIGHT

NOTES: _____

_____

_____

_____

_____

_____

_____

_____

_____

_____

_____

PHOTO DETAILS:

	LOCATION:	
SWIM:		
START DATE:	END DATE:	
TIME:	TIME:	
WEATHER:		
BAROMETER:		
AIR TEMP:	WATER TEMP:	℃
TIDE:	MOON:	J) 0

	RIG	BAIT
ROD 1:		
ROD2:		
ROD3:		
ROD4:		

DATE/TIME	ROD	BITE	FISH	WEIGHT

NOTES: _____

_____

_____

_____

_____

_____

_____

_____

_____

_____

_____

_____

PHOTO DETAILS:

	LOCATION:	
SWIM:		
START DATE:	END DATE:	
TIME:	TIME:	
WEATHER:		
BAROMETER:		
AIR TEMP:	WATER TEMP:	CC
TIDE:	MOON:	J) 0

	RIG	BAIT
ROD 1:		
ROD2:		
ROD3:		
ROD4:		

DATE/TIME	ROD	BITE	FISH	WEIGHT

NOTES: _____

_____

_____

_____

_____

_____

_____

_____

_____

_____

_____

_____

PHOTO DETAILS:

LOCATION:		
SWIM:		
START DATE:	END DATE:	
TIME:	TIME:	
WEATHER:		
BAROMETER:		
AIR TEMP:	WATER TEMP:	℃
TIDE:	MOON:	J) 0

	RIG	BAIT
ROD 1:		
ROD2:		
ROD3:		
ROD4:		

DATE/TIME	ROD	BITE	FISH	WEIGHT

NOTES:

PHOTO DETAILS:

	LOCATION:	
SWIM:		
START DATE:	END DATE:	
TIME:	TIME:	
WEATHER:		
BAROMETER:		
AIR TEMP:	WATER TEMP:	℃
TIDE:	MOON:	J) 0

	RIG	BAIT
ROD 1:		
ROD2:		
ROD3:		
ROD4:		

DATE/TIME	ROD	BITE	FISH	WEIGHT

NOTES: _____

_____

_____

_____

_____

_____

_____

_____

_____

_____

_____

_____

_____

PHOTO DETAILS:

	LOCATION:	
SWIM:		
START DATE:		END DATE:
TIME:		TIME:
WEATHER:		
BAROMETER:		
AIR TEMP:		WATER TEMP: ℃
TIDE:		MOON: J) 0

	RIG	BAIT
ROD 1:		
ROD2:		
ROD3:		
ROD4:		

DATE/TIME	ROD	BITE	FISH	WEIGHT

NOTES: _____

_____

_____

_____

_____

_____

_____

_____

_____

_____

_____

_____

PHOTO DETAILS:

LOCATION:		
SWIM:		
START DATE:	END DATE:	
TIME:	TIME:	
WEATHER:		
BAROMETER:		
AIR TEMP:	WATER TEMP:	℃
TIDE:	MOON:	J) 0

	RIG	BAIT
ROD 1:		
ROD2:		
ROD3:		
ROD4:		

DATE/TIME	ROD	BITE	FISH	WEIGHT

NOTES: _____

_____

_____

_____

_____

_____

_____

_____

_____

_____

_____

PHOTO DETAILS:

	LOCATION:	
SWIM:		
START DATE:	END DATE:	
TIME:	TIME:	
WEATHER:		
BAROMETER:		
AIR TEMP:	WATER TEMP:	CC
TIDE:	MOON:	J) 0

	RIG	BAIT
ROD 1:		
ROD2:		
ROD3:		
ROD4:		

DATE/TIME	ROD	BITE	FISH	WEIGHT

NOTES: _____

_____

_____

_____

_____

_____

_____

_____

_____

_____

_____

_____

PHOTO DETAILS:

	LOCATION:	
	SWIM:	

LOCATION:	
SWIM:	
START DATE:	END DATE:
TIME:	TIME:
WEATHER:	
BAROMETER:	
AIR TEMP:	WATER TEMP:	CC
TIDE:	MOON:	J) 0

	RIG	BAIT
ROD 1:		
ROD2:		
ROD3:		
ROD4:		

DATE/TIME	ROD	BITE	FISH	WEIGHT

NOTES: _____

_____

_____

_____

_____

_____

_____

_____

_____

_____

_____

_____

PHOTO DETAILS:

LOCATION:		
SWIM:		
START DATE:	END DATE:	
TIME:	TIME:	
WEATHER:		
BAROMETER:		
AIR TEMP:	WATER TEMP:	CC
TIDE:	MOON:	J) 0

	RIG	BAIT
ROD 1:		
ROD2:		
ROD3:		
ROD4:		

DATE/TIME	ROD	BITE	FISH	WEIGHT

NOTES:_____

_____

_____

_____

_____

_____

_____

_____

_____

_____

_____

PHOTO DETAILS:

	LOCATION:	
SWIM:		
START DATE:	END DATE:	
TIME:	TIME:	
WEATHER:		
BAROMETER:		
AIR TEMP:	WATER TEMP:	℃
TIDE:	MOON:	J) 0

	RIG	BAIT
ROD 1:		
ROD2:		
ROD3:		
ROD4:		

DATE/TIME	ROD	BITE	FISH	WEIGHT

NOTES:_____

_____

_____

_____

_____

_____

_____

_____

_____

_____

_____

PHOTO DETAILS:

	LOCATION:	
	SWIM:	

LOCATION:	
SWIM:	
START DATE:	END DATE:
TIME:	TIME:
WEATHER:	
BAROMETER:	
AIR TEMP:	WATER TEMP: ℃
TIDE:	MOON: J) 0

	RIG	BAIT
ROD 1:		
ROD2:		
ROD3:		
ROD4:		

DATE/TIME	ROD	BITE	FISH	WEIGHT

NOTES:_____

_____

_____

_____

_____

_____

_____

_____

_____

_____

_____

_____

PHOTO DETAILS:

	LOCATION:	
	SWIM:	

LOCATION:	
SWIM:	
START DATE:	END DATE:
TIME:	TIME:
WEATHER:	
BAROMETER:	
AIR TEMP:	WATER TEMP: °C
TIDE:	MOON: J) 0

	RIG	BAIT
ROD 1:		
ROD2:		
ROD3:		
ROD4:		

DATE/TIME	ROD	BITE	FISH	WEIGHT

NOTES: _____

_____

_____

_____

_____

_____

_____

_____

_____

_____

_____

PHOTO DETAILS:

	LOCATION:	
SWIM:		
START DATE:	END DATE:	
TIME:	TIME:	
WEATHER:		
BAROMETER:		
AIR TEMP:	WATER TEMP:	℃
TIDE:	MOON:	J) 0

	RIG	BAIT
ROD 1:		
ROD2:		
ROD3:		
ROD4:		

DATE/TIME	ROD	BITE	FISH	WEIGHT

NOTES:_____

_____

_____

_____

_____

_____

_____

_____

_____

_____

_____

_____

PHOTO DETAILS:

	LOCATION:	
SWIM:		
START DATE:	END DATE:	
TIME:	TIME:	
WEATHER:		
BAROMETER:		
AIR TEMP:	WATER TEMP:	CC
TIDE:	MOON: J) 0	

	RIG	BAIT
ROD 1:		
ROD2:		
ROD3:		
ROD4:		

DATE/TIME	ROD	BITE	FISH	WEIGHT

NOTES: _____

_____

_____

_____

_____

_____

_____

_____

_____

_____

_____

_____

PHOTO DETAILS:

LOCATION:		
SWIM:		
START DATE:	END DATE:	
TIME:	TIME:	
WEATHER:		
BAROMETER:		
AIR TEMP:	WATER TEMP:	CC
TIDE:	MOON: J) 0	

	RIG	BAIT
ROD 1:		
ROD2:		
ROD3:		
ROD4:		

DATE/TIME	ROD	BITE	FISH	WEIGHT

NOTES: _____

_____

_____

_____

_____

_____

_____

_____

_____

_____

PHOTO DETAILS:

LOCATION:	
SWIM:	
START DATE:	END DATE:
TIME:	TIME:
WEATHER:	
BAROMETER:	
AIR TEMP:	WATER TEMP: ℃
TIDE:	MOON: J) 0

	RIG	BAIT
ROD 1:		
ROD2:		
ROD3:		
ROD4:		

DATE/TIME	ROD	BITE	FISH	WEIGHT

NOTES:_____

_____

_____

_____

_____

_____

_____

_____

_____

_____

_____

_____

PHOTO DETAILS:

LOCATION:	
SWIM:	
START DATE:	END DATE:
TIME:	TIME:
WEATHER:	
BAROMETER:	
AIR TEMP:	WATER TEMP: CC
TIDE:	MOON: J) 0

	RIG	BAIT
ROD 1:		
ROD2:		
ROD3:		
ROD4:		

DATE/TIME	ROD	BITE	FISH	WEIGHT

NOTES: _____

_____

_____

_____

_____

_____

_____

_____

_____

_____

_____

_____

PHOTO DETAILS:

LOCATION:		
SWIM:		
START DATE:	END DATE:	
TIME:	TIME:	
WEATHER:		
BAROMETER:		
AIR TEMP:	WATER TEMP:	℃
TIDE:	MOON:	J) 0

	RIG	BAIT
ROD 1:		
ROD2:		
ROD3:		
ROD4:		

DATE/TIME	ROD	BITE	FISH	WEIGHT

NOTES: _____

_____

_____

_____

_____

_____

_____

_____

_____

_____

_____

PHOTO DETAILS:

LOCATION:	
SWIM:	
START DATE:	END DATE:
TIME:	TIME:
WEATHER:	
BAROMETER:	
AIR TEMP:	WATER TEMP: CC
TIDE:	MOON: J) 0

	RIG	BAIT
ROD 1:		
ROD2:		
ROD3:		
ROD4:		

DATE/TIME	ROD	BITE	FISH	WEIGHT

NOTES: _____

_____

_____

_____

_____

_____

_____

_____

_____

_____

_____

PHOTO DETAILS:

LOCATION:	
SWIM:	
START DATE:	END DATE:
TIME:	TIME:
WEATHER:	
BAROMETER:	
AIR TEMP:	WATER TEMP: ℃
TIDE:	MOON: J) 0

	RIG	BAIT
ROD 1:		
ROD2:		
ROD3:		
ROD4:		

DATE/TIME	ROD	BITE	FISH	WEIGHT

NOTES: _____

_____

_____

_____

_____

_____

_____

_____

_____

_____

_____

_____

PHOTO DETAILS:

	LOCATION:	
SWIM:		
START DATE:	END DATE:	
TIME:	TIME:	
WEATHER:		
BAROMETER:		
AIR TEMP:	WATER TEMP:	CC
TIDE:	MOON: J) 0	

	RIG	BAIT
ROD 1:		
ROD2:		
ROD3:		
ROD4:		

DATE/TIME	ROD	BITE	FISH	WEIGHT

NOTES:_____

_____

_____

_____

_____

_____

_____

_____

_____

_____

_____

PHOTO DETAILS:

LOCATION:		
SWIM:		
START DATE:	END DATE:	
TIME:	TIME:	
WEATHER:		
BAROMETER:		
AIR TEMP:	WATER TEMP:	℃
TIDE:	MOON:	J) 0

	RIG	BAIT
ROD 1:		
ROD2:		
ROD3:		
ROD4:		

DATE/TIME	ROD	BITE	FISH	WEIGHT

NOTES: _____

_____

_____

_____

_____

_____

_____

_____

_____

_____

_____

PHOTO DETAILS:

	LOCATION:	

LOCATION:	
SWIM:	
START DATE:	END DATE:
TIME:	TIME:
WEATHER:	
BAROMETER:	
AIR TEMP:	WATER TEMP: CC
TIDE:	MOON: J) 0

	RIG	BAIT
ROD 1:		
ROD2:		
ROD3:		
ROD4:		

DATE/TIME	ROD	BITE	FISH	WEIGHT

NOTES: _____

_____

_____

_____

_____

_____

_____

_____

_____

_____

_____

_____

PHOTO DETAILS:

LOCATION:		
SWIM:		
START DATE:	END DATE:	
TIME:	TIME:	
WEATHER:		
BAROMETER:		
AIR TEMP:	WATER TEMP:	℃
TIDE:	MOON:	J) 0

	RIG	BAIT
ROD 1:		
ROD2:		
ROD3:		
ROD4:		

DATE/TIME	ROD	BITE	FISH	WEIGHT

NOTES: _____

_____

_____

_____

_____

_____

_____

_____

_____

_____

_____

_____

PHOTO DETAILS:

LOCATION:	
SWIM:	
START DATE:	END DATE:
TIME:	TIME:
WEATHER:	
BAROMETER:	
AIR TEMP:	WATER TEMP: ℃
TIDE:	MOON: J) 0

	RIG	BAIT
ROD 1:		
ROD2:		
ROD3:		
ROD4:		

DATE/TIME	ROD	BITE	FISH	WEIGHT

NOTES:_____

_____

_____

_____

_____

_____

_____

_____

_____

_____

_____

PHOTO DETAILS:

LOCATION:	
SWIM:	
START DATE:	END DATE:
TIME:	TIME:
WEATHER:	
BAROMETER:	
AIR TEMP:	WATER TEMP: ℃
TIDE:	MOON: J) 0

	RIG	BAIT
ROD 1:		
ROD2:		
ROD3:		
ROD4:		

DATE/TIME	ROD	BITE	FISH	WEIGHT

NOTES: _____

_____

_____

_____

_____

_____

_____

_____

_____

_____

_____

_____

PHOTO DETAILS:

LOCATION:		
SWIM:		
START DATE:	END DATE:	
TIME:	TIME:	
WEATHER:		
BAROMETER:		
AIR TEMP:	WATER TEMP:	℃
TIDE:	MOON: J) 0	

	RIG	BAIT
ROD 1:		
ROD2:		
ROD3:		
ROD4:		

DATE/TIME	ROD	BITE	FISH	WEIGHT

NOTES: _____

_____

_____

_____

_____

_____

_____

_____

_____

_____

_____

PHOTO DETAILS:

LOCATION:	
SWIM:	
START DATE:	END DATE:
TIME:	TIME:
WEATHER:	
BAROMETER:	
AIR TEMP:	WATER TEMP: CC
TIDE:	MOON: J) 0

	RIG	BAIT
ROD 1:		
ROD2:		
ROD3:		
ROD4:		

DATE/TIME	ROD	BITE	FISH	WEIGHT

NOTES:_____

_____

_____

_____

_____

_____

_____

_____

_____

_____

_____

PHOTO DETAILS:

	LOCATION:	
	SWIM:	

START DATE:	END DATE:	
TIME:	TIME:	
WEATHER:		
BAROMETER:		
AIR TEMP:	WATER TEMP:	CC
TIDE:	MOON: J) 0	

	RIG	BAIT
ROD 1:		
ROD2:		
ROD3:		
ROD4:		

DATE/TIME	ROD	BITE	FISH	WEIGHT

NOTES:_____

_____

_____

_____

_____

_____

_____

_____

_____

_____

_____

_____

PHOTO DETAILS:

LOCATION:	
SWIM:	
START DATE:	END DATE:
TIME:	TIME:
WEATHER:	
BAROMETER:	
AIR TEMP:	WATER TEMP: CC
TIDE:	MOON: J) 0

	RIG	BAIT
ROD 1:		
ROD2:		
ROD3:		
ROD4:		

DATE/TIME	ROD	BITE	FISH	WEIGHT

NOTES:_____

_____

_____

_____

_____

_____

_____

_____

_____

_____

_____

PHOTO DETAILS:

LOCATION:	
SWIM:	
START DATE:	END DATE:
TIME:	TIME:
WEATHER:	
BAROMETER:	
AIR TEMP:	WATER TEMP: ℃
TIDE:	MOON: J) 0

	RIG	BAIT
ROD 1:		
ROD2:		
ROD3:		
ROD4:		

DATE/TIME	ROD	BITE	FISH	WEIGHT

NOTES: _____

_____

_____

_____

_____

_____

_____

_____

_____

_____

_____

_____

PHOTO DETAILS:

	LOCATION:	
	SWIM:	
START DATE:		END DATE:
TIME:		TIME:
	WEATHER:	
	BAROMETER:	
AIR TEMP:		WATER TEMP: ℃
TIDE:		MOON: J) 0

	RIG	BAIT
ROD 1:		
ROD2:		
ROD3:		
ROD4:		

DATE/TIME	ROD	BITE	FISH	WEIGHT

NOTES: _____

_____

_____

_____

_____

_____

_____

_____

_____

_____

_____

PHOTO DETAILS:

LOCATION:		
SWIM:		
START DATE:	END DATE:	
TIME:	TIME:	
WEATHER:		
BAROMETER:		
AIR TEMP:	WATER TEMP:	℃
TIDE:	MOON: J) 0	

	RIG	BAIT
ROD 1:		
ROD2:		
ROD3:		
ROD4:		

DATE/TIME	ROD	BITE	FISH	WEIGHT

NOTES:_____

_____

_____

_____

_____

_____

_____

_____

_____

_____

_____

PHOTO DETAILS:

	LOCATION:	
	SWIM:	
START DATE:	END DATE:
TIME:	TIME:
	WEATHER:	
	BAROMETER:	
AIR TEMP:	WATER TEMP: ℃
TIDE:	MOON: J) 0

	RIG	BAIT
ROD 1:		
ROD2:		
ROD3:		
ROD4:		

DATE/TIME	ROD	BITE	FISH	WEIGHT

NOTES:_____

_____

_____

_____

_____

_____

_____

_____

_____

_____

_____

_____

PHOTO DETAILS:

LOCATION:	
SWIM:	
START DATE:	END DATE:
TIME:	TIME:
WEATHER:	
BAROMETER:	
AIR TEMP:	WATER TEMP: ℃
TIDE:	MOON: J) O

	RIG	BAIT
ROD 1:		
ROD2:		
ROD3:		
ROD4:		

DATE/TIME	ROD	BITE	FISH	WEIGHT

NOTES:_____

_____

_____

_____

_____

_____

_____

_____

_____

_____

_____

PHOTO DETAILS:

	LOCATION:		
SWIM:			
START DATE:		END DATE:	
TIME:		TIME:	
WEATHER:			
BAROMETER:			
AIR TEMP:		WATER TEMP:	CC
TIDE:		MOON:	J) 0

	RIG	BAIT
ROD 1:		
ROD2:		
ROD3:		
ROD4:		

DATE/TIME	ROD	BITE	FISH	WEIGHT

NOTES: _____

_____

_____

_____

_____

_____

_____

_____

_____

_____

_____

PHOTO DETAILS:

LOCATION:	
SWIM:	
START DATE:	END DATE:
TIME:	TIME:
WEATHER:	
BAROMETER:	
AIR TEMP:	WATER TEMP: ℃
TIDE:	MOON: J) 0

	RIG	BAIT
ROD 1:		
ROD2:		
ROD3:		
ROD4:		

DATE/TIME	ROD	BITE	FISH	WEIGHT

NOTES: _____

_____

_____

_____

_____

_____

_____

_____

_____

_____

_____

_____

PHOTO DETAILS:

	LOCATION:			

LOCATION:	
SWIM:	
START DATE:	END DATE:
TIME:	TIME:
WEATHER:	
BAROMETER:	
AIR TEMP:	WATER TEMP: ℃
TIDE:	MOON: J) 0

	RIG	BAIT
ROD 1:		
ROD2:		
ROD3:		
ROD4:		

DATE/TIME	ROD	BITE	FISH	WEIGHT

NOTES: _____

_____

_____

_____

_____

_____

_____

_____

_____

_____

_____

_____

PHOTO DETAILS:

	LOCATION:	
SWIM:		
START DATE:	END DATE:	
TIME:	TIME:	
WEATHER:		
BAROMETER:		
AIR TEMP:	WATER TEMP:	CC
TIDE:	MOON: J) 0	

	RIG	BAIT
ROD 1:		
ROD2:		
ROD3:		
ROD4:		

DATE/TIME	ROD	BITE	FISH	WEIGHT

NOTES:_____

_____

_____

_____

_____

_____

_____

_____

_____

_____

_____

_____

PHOTO DETAILS:

		LOCATION:	

LOCATION:	
SWIM:	

START DATE:	END DATE:
TIME:	TIME:

WEATHER:	
BAROMETER:	

AIR TEMP:	WATER TEMP:	CC

TIDE:	MOON:	J) 0

	RIG	BAIT
ROD 1:		
ROD2:		
ROD3:		
ROD4:		

DATE/TIME	ROD	BITE	FISH	WEIGHT

NOTES: _____

_____

_____

_____

_____

_____

_____

_____

_____

_____

_____

_____

PHOTO DETAILS:

LOCATION:	
SWIM:	
START DATE:	END DATE:
TIME:	TIME:
WEATHER:	
BAROMETER:	
AIR TEMP:	WATER TEMP: ℃
TIDE:	MOON: J) 0

	RIG	BAIT
ROD 1:		
ROD2:		
ROD3:		
ROD4:		

DATE/TIME	ROD	BITE	FISH	WEIGHT

NOTES: _____

_____

_____

_____

_____

_____

_____

_____

_____

_____

_____

_____

PHOTO DETAILS:

LOCATION:		
SWIM:		
START DATE:	END DATE:	
TIME:	TIME:	
WEATHER:		
BAROMETER:		
AIR TEMP:	WATER TEMP:	℃
TIDE:	MOON:	J) 0

	RIG	BAIT
ROD 1:		
ROD2:		
ROD3:		
ROD4:		

DATE/TIME	ROD	BITE	FISH	WEIGHT

NOTES:_____

_____

_____

_____

_____

_____

_____

_____

_____

_____

_____

PHOTO DETAILS:

	RIG	BAIT

LOCATION:

SWIM:

START DATE:	END DATE:
TIME:	TIME:

WEATHER:

BAROMETER:

AIR TEMP:	WATER TEMP:	CC
TIDE:	MOON: J) 0	

	RIG	BAIT
ROD 1:		
ROD2:		
ROD3:		
ROD4:		

DATE/TIME	ROD	BITE	FISH	WEIGHT

NOTES: _____

_____

_____

_____

_____

_____

_____

_____

_____

_____

_____

_____

PHOTO DETAILS:

LOCATION:	
SWIM:	
START DATE:	END DATE:
TIME:	TIME:
WEATHER:	
BAROMETER:	
AIR TEMP:	WATER TEMP: ℃
TIDE:	MOON: J) 0

	RIG	BAIT
ROD 1:		
ROD2:		
ROD3:		
ROD4:		

DATE/TIME	ROD	BITE	FISH	WEIGHT

NOTES:_____

_____

_____

_____

_____

_____

_____

_____

_____

_____

_____

PHOTO DETAILS:

	LOCATION:	
SWIM:		
START DATE:		END DATE:
TIME:		TIME:
WEATHER:		
BAROMETER:		
AIR TEMP:		WATER TEMP: ℃
TIDE:		MOON: J) 0

	RIG	BAIT
ROD 1:		
ROD2:		
ROD3:		
ROD4:		

DATE/TIME	ROD	BITE	FISH	WEIGHT

NOTES: _____

_____

_____

_____

_____

_____

_____

_____

_____

_____

_____

PHOTO DETAILS:

		LOCATION:			

LOCATION:	
SWIM:	

START DATE:	END DATE:
TIME:	TIME:

WEATHER:
BAROMETER:

AIR TEMP:	WATER TEMP:	CC
TIDE:	MOON: J) 0	

	RIG	BAIT
ROD 1:		
ROD2:		
ROD3:		
ROD4:		

DATE/TIME	ROD	BITE	FISH	WEIGHT

NOTES: _____

_____

_____

_____

_____

_____

_____

_____

_____

_____

_____

_____

PHOTO DETAILS:

	LOCATION:	
	SWIM:	

START DATE:	END DATE:	
TIME:	TIME:	
WEATHER:		
BAROMETER:		
AIR TEMP:	WATER TEMP:	℃
TIDE:	MOON:	J) 0

	RIG	BAIT
ROD 1:		
ROD2:		
ROD3:		
ROD4:		

DATE/TIME	ROD	BITE	FISH	WEIGHT

NOTES: _____

_____

_____

_____

_____

_____

_____

_____

_____

_____

_____

_____

PHOTO DETAILS:

	LOCATION:	
SWIM:		
START DATE:	END DATE:	
TIME:	TIME:	
WEATHER:		
BAROMETER:		
AIR TEMP:	WATER TEMP:	CC
TIDE:	MOON:	J) 0

	RIG	BAIT
ROD 1:		
ROD2:		
ROD3:		
ROD4:		

DATE/TIME	ROD	BITE	FISH	WEIGHT

NOTES:_____

_____

_____

_____

_____

_____

_____

_____

_____

_____

_____

PHOTO DETAILS:

LOCATION:		
SWIM:		
START DATE:	END DATE:	
TIME:	TIME:	
WEATHER:		
BAROMETER:		
AIR TEMP:	WATER TEMP:	℃
TIDE:	MOON:	J) 0

	RIG	BAIT
ROD 1:		
ROD2:		
ROD3:		
ROD4:		

DATE/TIME	ROD	BITE	FISH	WEIGHT

NOTES: _____

_____

_____

_____

_____

_____

_____

_____

_____

_____

_____

PHOTO DETAILS:

Made in the USA
Las Vegas, NV
27 February 2021

18686173R00069